GREGORY CORSO

GASOLINE
&
THE VESTAL LADY ON BRATTLE

CITY LIGHTS BOOKS · SAN FRANCISCO

GASOLINE
© 1958 by Gregory Corso

THE VESTAL LADY ON BRATTLE
© 1955 by Gregory Corso

Cover design by Rex Ray

ISBN 10: 0-87286-088-4

ISBN 13: 978-0-87286-088-9

The Vestal Lady on Brattle was first published by Richard Brukenfeld, Cambridge, Massachusetts in 1955.

Some of these poems appeared in *The Cambridge Review, Contact, Audience, The Harvard Advocate, Esquire, Evergreen Review, The Pelican, World Telegram and Sun*, and *Partisan Review.*

Visit our website: <u>www.citylights.com</u>

CITY LIGHTS BOOKS are edited by Lawrence Ferlinghetti and Nancy J. Peters and published at the City Lights Bookstore, 261 Columbus Avenue, San Francisco, CA 94133.

CONTENTS

GASOLINE

THE VESTAL LADY ON BRATTLE

GASOLINE

I dedicate this book to the angels of Clinton Prison who, in my 17th year, handed me, from all the cells surrounding me, books of illumination.

G.C.

". . . It comes, I tell you, immense with gasolined rags and bits of wire and old bent nails, a dark arriviste, from a dark river within."

Gregory Corso, *How Poetry Comes to Me*

INTRODUCTION

Open this book as you would a box of crazy toys, take in your hands a refinement of beauty out of a destructive atmosphere. These combinations are imaginary and pure, in accordance with Corso's individual (therefore universal) DESIRE.

All his own originality! What's his connection, but his own beauty? Such weird haiku-like juxtapositions aren't in the American book. Ah! but the real classic tradition—from Aristotle's description of metaphor to the wildness of his Shelley—and Apollinaire, Lorca, Mayakovsky. Corso is a great word-slinger, first naked sign of a poet, a scientific master of mad mouthfuls of language. He wants a surface hilarious with ellipses, jumps of the strangest phrasing picked off the streets of his mind like "mad children of soda caps."

This is his great *sound*: "O drop that fire engine out of your mouth!"

Crazier: "Dirty Ears aims a knife at me, I pump him full of lost watches."

What nerve! "You, Mexico, you have no Chicago, no white-blonde moll." ("H. G. Wells," unpublished.)

He gets pure abstract poetry, the inside sound of language alone.

But what is he *saying*? Who cares?! It's said! "Outside by a Halloween fire, wise on a charred log, an old man is dictating to the heir of the Goon."

This heir sometimes transcribes perfect modern lyrics anyone can dig: "Italian Extravaganza," "Birthplace Revisited," "Last Gangster," "Mad Yak," "Furnished Room," "Haarlem," "Last Night I Drove a Car," Ecce Homo," "Hello."

A rare sad goonish knowledge with reality—a hip piss on reality also—he prefers his dreams. Why not? His Heaven is Poetry. He explains at length in the great unpublished "Power":

> I do not sing of dictatorial power.
> The stiff arm of dictatorship is symbolic of awful power.
> In my room I have gathered enough gasoline and evidence to allow dictators inexhaustible power.
> Am I the stiff arm of Costa Rica?
> Do I wear red and green in Chrysler Squads?
> Do I hate my people?
> Will they forgive me their taxes?
> Am I to be shot at the racetrack? Do they plot now?
> . . . .
> Beautiful people, you too are power. I remember your power.
> I have not forgotten you in the snows of Bavaria skiing down on the sleeping village with flares and carbines,
> I have not forgotten you rubbing your greasy hands on my aircraft, signing your obscure names on the blockbuster!

No!

I have not forgotten the bazooka you decked with palm
    fastened on the shoulder of a black man aimed at a
    tank full of Aryans!

Nor have I forgotten the grenade, the fear and emer-
    gency it spread throughout your brother's trench.

You are power, beautiful people!

. . . .

Power is not to be dropped from a plane

A hat is power

The world is power

Being afraid is power

Standing on a streetcorner waiting for no one is power

The demon is not as powerful as walking across the
    street

The angel is not as powerful as looking and then not
    looking.

What a solitary dignitary! He's got the angelic power of
making autonomous poems, like god making brooks.

"With me automaticism is an entranced moment in which
the mind accelerates a constant hour of mind-foolery, mind-
genius, mind-madness . . .

"When Bird Parker or Miles Davis blow a standard piece of
music, they break off into other own-self little unstandard
sounds—well, that's my way with poetry— X Y & Z, call it
automatic—I call it a standard flow (because at the offset
words are standard) that is intentionally distracted diversed

into my own sound. Of course many will say a poem written on that order is unpolished, etc.—that's just what I want them to be—because I have made them truly my own— which is inevitably something NEW—like all good spontaneous jazz, newness is acceptable and expected—by hip people who listen."

"Don't Shoot The Warthog!" The mind has taken a leap in language. He curses like a brook, pure poetry. "I screamed the name: Beauty!" We're the fabled damned if we put it down. He's probably the greatest poet in America, and he's starving in Europe.

ALLEN GINSBERG
Amsterdam, Holland Oct 57

ODE TO COIT TOWER

O anti-verdurous phallic were't not for your pouring height
    looming in tears like a sick tree or your ever-gaudy-
    comfort jabbing your city's much wrinkled sky you'd
    seem an absurd Babel squatting before mortal millions
Because I filled your dull sockets with my New York City
    eyes vibrations that hadn't doomed dumb Empire State
    did not doom thee
Enough my eyes made you see phantasmal at night mad
    children of soda caps laying down their abundant blond
    verse on the gridiron of each other's eucharistic feet like
    distant kings laying down treasures from camels
Illuminations hinged to masculine limbs fresh with the labor
    sweat of cablecar & Genoa papa pushcart
Bounty of electricity & visions carpented on pig-bastard night
    in its spore like the dim lights of some hallucinating
    facade
Ah tower from thy berryless head I'd a vision in common
    with myself the proximity of Alcatraz and not the hip
    volley of white jazz & verse or verse & jazz embraced
    but a real heart-rending constant vision of Alcatraz
    marshalled before my eyes
Stocky Alcatraz weeping on Neptune's table whose petrific
    bondage crushes the dreamless seaharp gasping for song
    O that that piece of sea fails to dream
Tower I'd a verdure vagueness fixed by a green wind the

shade of Mercy lashed with cold nails against the
wheatweather Western sky weeping I'm sure for hu-
manity's vast door to open that all men be free that
both hinge and lock die that all doors if they close close
like Chinese bells

Was it man's love to screw the sky with monuments span the
bay with orange & silver bridges shuttling structure into
structure incorruptible in this endless tie each age
impassions be it in stone or steel either in echo or
half-heard ruin

Was it man's love that put that rock there never to avalanche
but in vision or this imaginary now or myself standing
on Telegraph Hill Nob Hill Russian Hill the same view
always Alcatraz like a deserted holiday

And I cried for Alcatraz there in your dumb hollows O tower
clenching my Pan's foot with vivid hoard of Dannemora

Cried for that which was no longer sovereign in me stinking
of dead dreams dreams I yet feign to bury thus to shun
reality's worm

Dreams that once jumped joyous bright from my heart like
sparks issued from a wild sharper's wheel now issued no
longer

Were't not for cities or prisons O tower I might yet be that
verdure monk lulling over green country albums with no
greater dream than my youth's dream

Eyes of my hands! Queen Penthesileia and her tribe! Mes-
senger stars Doctor Deformous back from his leprosy
and woe! Thracian ships! Joyprints of pure air!

Impossible for me to betray even the simplest tree

Idiotic colossus I came to your city during summer after
      Cambridge there also no leaf throbbed between my
      fingers no cool insect thrilled my palm though I'd a
      vision there Death seated like a huge black stove

Inspired by such I came to your city walked Market Street
      singing hark hark the dogs do bark the beggars are
      coming to town and ran mad across Golden Gate into
      Sausalito and fell exhausted in a field where an endless
      scarecrow lay its head on my lap

How happily mad I was O tower lying there amid gossipy
      green dreaming of Quetzalcoatl as I arched my back like
      a rainbow over some imaginary gulph

O for that madness again that infinitive solitude where illu-
      sion spoke Truth's divine dialect

I should have stayed yet I left to Mexico to Quetzalcoatl and
      heard there atop Teotihuacan in T-prophetic-Cuauhxi-
      calli-voice a dark anthem for the coming year

Ah tower tower that I felt sad for Alcatraz and not for your
      heroes lessened not the tourist love of my eyes

I saw your blackjacketed saints your Zens potsmokers
      Athenians and cocksmen

Though the West Wind seemed to harbor there not one
      pure Shelleyean dream of let's say hay-
          like universe
            golden heap on a wall of fire
      sprinting toward the gauzy eradication of
          Swindleresque Ink

IN THE FLEETING HAND OF TIME

On the steps of the bright madhouse
I hear the bearded bell shaking down the woodlawn
the final knell of my world
I climb and enter a firey gathering of knights
they unaware of my presence lay forth sheepskin plans
and with mailcoated fingers trace my arrival
back back back when on the black steps of Nero lyre Rome
    I stood
in my arms the wailing philosopher
the final call of mad history
Now my presence is known
my arrival marked by illuminated stains
The great windows of Paradise open
Down to radiant dust fall the curtains of Past Time
In fly flocks of multicolored birds
Light winged light O the wonder of light
Time takes me by the hand
born March 26 1930 I am led 100 mph o'er the vast market
    of choice
what to choose? what to choose?
O — — — and I leave my orange room of myth
no chance to lock away my toys of Zeus
I choose the room of Bleecker Street
A baby mother stuffs my mouth with a pale Milanese breast
I suck I struggle I cry O Olympian mother

unfamiliar this breast to me
Snows
Decade of icy asphalt doomed horses
Weak dreams   Dark corridors of P.S.42   Roofs   Ratthroated
     pigeons
Led 100 mph over these all too real Mafia streets
profanely I shed my Hermean wings
O Time be merciful
throw me beneath your humanity of cars
feed me to giant grey skyscrapers
exhaust my heart to your bridges
I discard my lyre of Orphic futility

And for such betrayal I climb these bright mad steps
and enter this room of paradisical light
ephemeral
Time
a long long dog having chased its orbited tail
comes grab my hand
and leads me into conditional life

VISION OF ROTTERDAM

      September 1957 summoned by my vision-agent
via ventriloquial telegram
delivered by the dumb mouths stoned upon Notre Dame
      given golden fare & 17th Century diagram
I left the gargoyle city
And
Two suitcases filled with despair
      arrived in Rotterdam

Rotterdam is dying again
      steamers & tankers
    unload an awful sight
May 1940 stevedores lead forth a platoon of leukemia
Pleasure ships send metalvoiced rats teeheeing a propaganda
    of ruin
A cargo of scream deafens the tinhorn of feeble War
Bombers overhead
      Young blond children in white blouses
      crawl in the streets gnawing their houses
The old the sick the mad leave their wheelchairs & cells and
    kneel in adoration before the gentle torpedo of miracles
Bombers unanswerable to the heart
      vitalize a Sunday afternoon dream
Bombs like jewels surprise
Explosion explosion explosion

Avalanche on medieval stilts brought down 1940
Mercy leans against her favorite bombardment
              and forgives the bomb

Alone
Eyes on the antique diagram
    I wander down the ruin and see
        amid a madness of coughing bicycles
the scheme of a new Rotterdam humming in the vacancy

2 WEIRD HAPPENINGS IN HAARLEM

1

Four windmills, acquaintanceships,
were spied one morning eating tulips.
Noon
and the entire city flips
screaming: Apocalypse! Apocalypse!

2

O people! my people!
something weirdly architectural
like a rackety cannibal
came to Haarlem last night
and ate up a canal!

24

THE LAST WARMTH OF ARNOLD

Arnold, warm with God,
hides beneath the porch
remembering the time of escape, imprisoned in Vermont,
shoveling snow. Arnold was from somewhere else,
where it was warm; where he wore suede shoes
and played ping-pong.
Arnold knew the Koran.
And he knew to sing:
>   Young Julien Sorel
>   Knew his Latin well
>   And was wise as he
>   Was beautiful
>   Until his head fell.

In the empty atmosphere
Arnold kept a tiplet pigeon, a bag of chicken corn.
He thought of Eleanor, her hands;
watched her sit sad in school
He got Carmine to lure her into the warm atmosphere;
he wanted to kiss her, live with her forever;
break her head with bargains.

Who is Arnold? Well,
I first saw him wear a black cap
covered with old Wilkie buttons. He was 13.

And afraid. But with a smile. And he was always
willing to walk you home, to meet your mother,
to tell her about Hester Street Park
about the cold bums there;
about the cold old Jewish ladies who sat,
hands folded, sad, keeping their faces
away from the old Jewish Home.
Arnold grew up with a knowledge of bookies
and chicken pluckers

And Arnold knew to sing:
      Dead now my 15th year
      F.D.R., whose smiling face
      Made evil the buck-toothed Imperialist,
      The moustached Aryan,
      The jut-jawed Caesar—
      Dead now, and I weep . . .
      For once I did hate that man
      and no reason
      but innocent hate
      —my cap decked with old Wilkie buttons.

Arnold was kicked in the balls
by an Italian girl who got mad
because there was a big coal strike on
and it forced the Educational Alliance to close its doors.
Arnold, weak and dying, stole pennies from the library,
but he also read about Paderewski.

He used to walk along South Street
wondering about the various kinds of glue.
And it was about airplane glue he was thinking
when he fell and died beneath the Brooklyn Bridge.

AMNESIA IN MEMPHIS

Who am I, flat beneath the shades of Isis,
This clay-skinned body, made study
by the physicians of Memphis?
Was it always my leaving the North
Snug on the back of the crocodile?
Do I remember this whorl of mummy cloth
As I stood fuming by the Nile?
O life abandoned! half-embalmed, I beat the soil!
For what I am; who I am, I cannot regain,
Nor sponge my life back with the charm of Ibis oil—
Still-omen of the dribbling Scarab!
Fate that leads me into the chamber of blue perfumes!
Is there no other worthy of prophecy
Than that Decker who decks my spine with ostrick plumes?

No more will the scurvy Sphinx
With beggy prophets their prophecies relate—
The papyrus readers have seen the Falcon's head
Fall unto the Jackal's plate.

MEXICAN IMPRESSIONS

I

Through a moving window
I see a glimpse of burros
 a Pepsi Cola stand,
an old Indian sitting
 smiling toothless by a hut.

II

Stopping at Guaymas,
a brand new Ford pick-up
filled with melancholy laborers;
in the driver's seat, a young child
—doomed by his sombrero.

III

Windmill, silverwooded, slatless, motionless in Mexico—
Birdlike incongruous windmill, like a broken crane,
One-legged, stiff, arbitrary, with wide watchful eye,
How did you happen here?—All alone, alien, helpless,

Here where there is no wind?
Living gaunt structure resigned, are you pleased
    with this dry windless monkage?
Softer, the cactus outlives you.

IV

I tell you, Mexico—
I think miles and miles of dead full-bodied horses—
Thoroughbreds and work horses, flat on their sides
Stiffened with straight legs and lipless mouths.
It is the stiff leg, Mexico, the jutted tooth,
That wrecks my equestrian dreams of nightmare.

V

In the Mexican Zoo
    they have ordinary
American cows.

30

SUN

(*Automatic Poem*)

Sun hypnotic! holy ball protracted long and sure! firey
goblet! day-babble!
Sun, sun-webbed heat! tropic goblet dry! spider thirst! Sun,
unwater!
Sun misery sun ire sun sick sun dead sun rot sun relic!
Sun o'er Afric sky low and tipped, spilt, almost empty,
hollow vial, sunbone, sunstone, iron sun, sundial.
Sun dinosaur of electric motion extinct and fossiled, babble
on!
Sun, season of the season, catching actual sunfish, on the
green shore sunbathing like a madness.
Sun eros hellish superreal conglomeration of miasmatic ire!
Sun, sun-downed beings in desert life astounded, go down!
Sun circus! tent of helion, apollo, rha, sol, sun, exhult!
The sun like a blazing ship went down in Teliphicci lake.
The sun like a blazing disc of jelly slid over the Teliphiccian
alps.
The sun leads the night and follows the night and leads the
night.
The sun can be chariot-driven.
The sun like a blazing lollipop can be sucked.

The sun is shaped like a curved beckoning finger.
The sun spins walks dances skips runs.
The sun favors palm citrics tubercular-lungs
The sun eats up Teliphicci lake and alps every rising.
The sun does not know what it is to like or dislike.
The sun all my life went down in Teliphicci lake.
O constant hole where all beyond is true Byzantium.

PUMA IN CHAPULTEPEC ZOO

Long smooth slow swift soft cat
What score, whose choreography did you dance to
      when they pulled the final curtain down?
Can such ponderous grace remain
      here, all alone, on this 9x10 stage?
Will they give you another chance
      perhaps to dance the Sierras?
How sad you seem; looking at you
      I think of Ulanova
      locked in some small furnished room
      in New York, on East 17th Street
      in the Puerto Rican section.

BOTTICELLI'S "SPRING"

No sign of Spring!
Florentine sentinels
    from icy campanili
watch for a sign—
       Lorenzo dreams to awaken bluebirds
       Ariosto sucks his thumb.
       Michelangelo sits forward on his bed
       . . . awakened by no new change.
       Dante pulls back his velvet hood,
       his eyes are deep and sad.
       His great dane weeps.
No sign of Spring!
       Leonardo paces his unbearable room
       . . . holds an arrogant eye on die-hard snow.
       Raffaelo steps into a warm bath
          . . . his long silken hair is dry
       because of lack of sun.
       Aretino remembers Spring in Milan; his mother,
       who now, on sweet Milanese hills, sleeps.
No sign of Spring! No sign!
Ah, Botticelli opens the door of his studio.

ECCE HOMO

—painting by Theodoricus—

Inside the wounded hands and feet
the fragments of earlier wounds (almost healed)
like black almonds crusted
are answer enough—
the nails went thru the man to God.

The crown of thorns (a superb idea!)
and the sidewound (an atrocity!)
only penetrate the man.

I have seen many paintings of this;
the same inflictions,
subject of proof; *ecce signum*
the same sad face;
I have forgotten them all.
O Theodoricus, youth, vagueness, my fault; yet yours!
What grief! this
impossible to forget.

UCCELLO

They will never die on that battlefield
nor the shade of wolves recruit their hoard like brides of
wheat on all horizons   waiting there to consume battle's end
There will be no dead to tighten their loose bellies
no heap of starched horses to redsmash their bright eyes
or advance their eat of dead
They would rather hungersulk with mad tongues
than believe that on that field no man dies

They will never die who fight so embraced
breath to breath   eye knowing eye   impossible to die
or move   no light seeping through   no maced arm
nothing but horse outpanting horse   shield brilliant upon
shield   all made starry by the dot ray of a helmeted eye
ah   how difficult to fall between those knitted lances
And those banners! angry as to flush insignia across its
erasure of sky
You'd think he'd paint his armies by the coldest rivers
have rows of iron skulls flashing in the dark
You'd think it impossible for any man to die
each combatant's mouth is a castle of song
each iron fist a dreamy gong   flail resounding flail
like cries of gold
how I dream to join such battle!
a silver man on a black horse with red standard and striped
lance   never to die but to be endless
a golden prince of pictorial war

ON THE WALLS
OF A DULL FURNISHED ROOM

I hang old photos of my childhood girls—
with breaking heart I sit, elbow on table,
Chin on hand, studying
      the proud eyes of Helen,
      the weak mouth of Jane,
      the golden hair of Susan.

D. SCARLATTI

Scarlatti counts his breath with a nasty
                suicide wound;
He hip-hops in the sewer, a fiend
                to unlistened powers.
He wears a dress coat, a top hat; has a cane
                and goes hip-hop
thru demented halls.
    ears open for an old echo.

ITALIAN EXTRAVAGANZA

Mrs. Lombardi's month-old son is dead.
I saw it in Rizzo's funeral parlor,
A small purplish wrinkled head.

They've just finished having high mass for it;
They're coming out now
. . . wow, such a small coffin!
And ten black cadillacs to haul it in.

BIRTHPLACE REVISITED

I stand in the dark light in the dark street
and look up at my window, I was born there.
The lights are on; other people are moving about.
I am with raincoat; cigarette in mouth,
hat over eye, hand on gat.
I cross the street and enter the building.
The garbage cans haven't stopped smelling.
I walk up the first flight; Dirty Ears
aims a knife at me . . .
I pump him full of lost watches.

THE LAST GANGSTER

Waiting by the window
my feet enwrapped with the dead bootleggers of Chicago
I am the last gangster, safe, at last,
waiting by a bullet-proof window.

I look down the street and know
the two torpedoes from St. Louis.
I've watched them grow old
. . . guns rusting in their arthritic hands.

I MISS MY DEAR CATS

My water-colored hands are catless now
seated here alone in the dark
my window-shaped head is bowed with sad draperies
I am catless near death almost
behind me my last cat hanging on the wall
dead of my hand drink bloated
And on all my other walls from attic to cellar
my sad life of cats hangs

BUT I DO NOT NEED KINDNESS

I have known the strange nurses of Kindness,
I have seen them kiss the sick, attend the old,
give candy to the mad!
I have watched them, at night, dark and sad,
rolling wheelchairs by the sea!
I have known the fat pontiffs of Kindness,
the little old grey-haired lady,
the neighborhood priest,
the famous poet,
the mother,
I have known them all!
I have watched them, at night, dark and sad,
pasting posters of mercy
        on the stark posts of despair.

2

I have known Almighty Kindness Herself!
I have sat beside Her pure white feet,
gaining Her confidence!
We spoke of nothing unkind,
but one night I was tormented by those strange nurses,
those fat pontiffs
The little old lady rode a spiked car over my head!
The priest cut open my stomach, put his hands in me,

39

and cried:—Where's your soul? Where's your soul!—
The famous poet picked me up
and threw me out of the window!
The mother abandoned me!
I ran to Kindness, broke into Her chamber,
and profaned!
with an unnamable knife I gave Her a thousand wounds,
and inflicted them with filth!
I carried Her away, on my back, like a ghoul!
down the cobble-stoned night!
Dogs howled! Cats fled! All windows closed!
I carried Her ten flights of stairs!
Dropped Her on the floor of my small room,
and kneeling beside Her, I wept. I wept.

3

But what is Kindness? I have killed Kindness,
but what is it?
You are kind because you live a kind life.
St. Francis was kind.
The landlord is kind.
A cane is kind.
Can I say people, sitting in parks, are kinder?

DON'T SHOOT THE WARTHOG

A child came to me
swinging an ocean on a stick.
He told me his sister was dead,
I pulled down his pants
and gave him a kick.
I drove him down the streets
down the night of my generation
I screamed his name, his cursed name,
down the streets of my generation
and children lept in joy to the name
and running came.
Mothers and fathers bent their heads to hear;
I screamed the name.

The child trembled, fell,
and staggered up again,
I screamed his name!
And a fury of mothers and fathers
sank their teeth into his brain.
I called to the angels of my generation
on the rooftops, in the alleyways,
beneath the garbage and the stones,
I screamed the name! and they came
and gnawed the child's bones.

I AM 25

With a love a madness for Shelley
Chatterton   Rimbaud
and the needy-yap of my youth
          has gone from ear to ear:
       I HATE OLD POETMEN!
Especially old poetmen who retract
who consult other old poetmen
who speak their youth in whispers,
saying:—I did those then
          but that was then
          that was then—
O I would quiet old men
say to them:—I am your friend
               what you once were, thru me
               you'll be again—
Then at night in the confidence of their homes
rip out their apology-tongues
          and steal their poems.

TO A DOWNFALLEN ROSE

When I laid aside the verses of Mimnermus,
I lived a life of canned heat and raw hands,
alone, not far from my body did I wander,
walked with the hope of a sudden dreamy forest of gold.
O rose, downfallen, bend your huge vegetic back;
eye down the imposter sun . . . in winter dream
sulk your rosefamed head into the bile of golden giant,
ah, rose, augment the rose furtherstill!
Whence upon that self-created dive in Eden
you blossomed where the Watchmaker of Nothingness
    lulled,
your birth did cause bits of smashed night to pop,
causing my dreamy forest to unfold.
Yes, and the Watchmaker, his wheely-flesh
and jewelled-bones spoiled as he awoke,
and, in the face of your Somethingness, he fled
waving oblivious monks in his unwinded hands.
The sun cannot see upheaved spadics, the tennis of Venus
and the court of Mars sing the big lie of the sun,
ah, faraway ball of fur, sponge up the elements;
make clear the trees and the mountains of the earth,
arise and turn away from the vast fixedness.

Rose! Rose! my tinhorneared rose!
Rose is my visionic eyehand of all Mysticdom

Rose is my wise chair of bombed houses
Rose is my patient electric eyes, eyes, eyes, eyes,
Rose is my festive jowl,
Dali Lama Grand Vicar Glorious Caesar rose!

When I hear the rose scream
I gather all the failure experiments of an anatomical empire
and, with some chemical dream, discover
the hateful law of the earth and sun, and the screaming
        rose between.

THREE

1

The streetsinger is sick
crouched in the doorway, holding his heart.

One less song in the noisy night.

2

Outside the wall
the aged gardener plants his shears
A new young man
has come to snip the hedge

3

Death weeps because Death is human
spending all day in a movie when a child dies.

HELLO..

It is disastrous to be a wounded deer.
I'm the most wounded, wolves stalk,
and I have my failures, too.
My flesh is caught on the Inevitable Hook!
As a child I saw many things I did not want to be.
Am I the person I did not want to be?
That talks-to-himself person?
That neighbors-make-fun-of person?
Am I he who, on museum steps, sleeps on his side?
Do I wear the cloth of a man who has failed?
Am I the looney man?
In the great serenade of things,
        am I the most cancelled passage?

NO WORD

It is better man a word elongate
and eat up what another spake
for no man is word enough
who complains, to boot,
the word he ate was tasteless tough

It is better man give up his diction
become mouthless
it is better
that another man, myself,
heed his restriction

I know no word that is mine
and I am tired of his
It is better to sew his mouth
dynamite his ears hearless
drown his vocabulary

It is better
his eyes speak and listen as well as see

THE MAD YAK

I am watching them churn the last milk
    they'll ever get from me.
They are waiting for me to die;
They want to make buttons out of my bones.
Where are my sisters and brothers?
That tall monk there, loading my uncle,
    he has a new cap.
And that idiot student of his—
    I never saw that muffler before.
Poor uncle, he lets them load him.
How sad he is, how tired!
I wonder what they'll do with his bones?
And that beautiful tail!
How many shoelaces will they make of that!

THIS WAS MY MEAL

In the peas I saw upside down letters of MONK
And beside it, in the Eyestares of Wine
I saw Olive & Blackhair
    I decided sunset to dine

I cut through the cowbrain and saw Christmas
& my birthday run hand in hand in the snow
I cut deeper
    and Christmas bled to the edge of the plate

I turned to my father
    and he ate my birthday
I drank my milk and saw trees outrun themselves
    valleys outdo themselves
    and no mountain stood a chance of not walking

Dessert came in the spindly hands of stepmother
I wanted to drop fire-engines from my mouth!
But in ran the moonlight and grabbed the prunes.

FOR MILES

Your sound is faultless
      pure & round
          holy
      almost profound

Your sound is your sound
      true & from within
      a confession
      soulful & lovely

Poet whose sound is played
      lost or recorded
      but heard
      can you recall that 54 night at the Open Door
      when you & bird
      wailed five in the morning some wondrous
      yet unimaginable score?

DOLL POEM

A favorite doll
knows the pain of a child's farewell.
Buried in the crib in the attic it dies forever.
Candy-colors fade
long pants lead us elsewhere
and a child's hands are getting hair.
Chewed-pencils, clips, pennies in our pockets
where are they?
The child's body is longer
long as the earth
everybody walks on him, some on wheelchairs,
long mad envious journey.
Soda and fig-newtons will erupt from the mouth.

LAST NIGHT I DROVE A CAR

Last night I drove a car
        not knowing how to drive
        not owning a car
I drove and knocked down
        people I loved
        . . . went 120 through one town.

I stopped at Hedgeville
        and slept in the back seat
        . . . excited about my new life.

ZIZI'S LAMENT

I am in love with the laughing sickness
it would do me a lot of good if I had it—
I have worn the splendid gowns of Sudan,
carried the magnificent halivas of Boudodin Bros.,
kissed the singing Fatimas of the pimp of Aden,
wrote glorious psalms in Hakhaliba's cafe,
but I've never had the laughing sickness,
so what good am I?

The fat merchant offers me opium, kief, hashish,
        even camel juice,
all is unsatisfactory—
O bitter damned night! you again! must I yet
pluck out my unreal teeth
undress my unlaughable self
put to sleep this melancholy head?
I am nothing without the laughing sickness.

My father's got it, my grandfather had it;
surely my Uncle Fez will get it, but me, me
who it would do the most good,
will I ever get it?

PARIS

Childcity, Aprilcity,
Spirits of angels crouched in doorways,
Poets, worms in hair, beautiful Baudelaire,
Artaud, Rimbaud, Apollinaire,
Look to the nightcity—
Informers and concierges,
Montparnassian woe, deathical Notre Dame,
To the nightcircle look, dome heirloomed,
Hugo and Zola together entombed,
Harlequin deathtrap,
Seine generates ominous mud,
Eiffel looks down—sees the Apocalyptical ant crawl,
New Yorkless city,
City of Germans dead and gone,
Dollhouse of Mama War.

THE VESTAL LADY ON BRATTLE

INTRODUCTION

Corso's attitudes and subject matter range in apparently helter-skelter fashion throughout these pages. But the pot-pourri may nonetheless indicate to the reader that Corso's overall vision is a fundamentally organic one, a vision having deeply instinctive sources of vitality. His images, many of them recurring over and over again, have an irrepressible way of stamping these poems as Corso's, not "some young poet's," and the total unity thereby derived is one which many more consciously inventive poets never achieve. Corso, at his worst, cannot help himself, and the poem, always vigorous, runs away from him. But at his best, he achieves a clear-cut meaning without stiffening into the lifeless poet's state of rigor mortis. At such rare moments, he makes a lasting impression—he is simultaneously conscious yet remains fluidly child-like, which is no small achievement. *The Vestal Lady*, for example, is the product of such a balance.

P.L.B.

THE VESTAL LADY ON BRATTLE

Within a delicate grey ruin
the vestal lady on Brattle
is up at dawn, as is her custom,
with the raise of a shade.

Swan-boned slippers revamp her aging feet;
she glides within an outer room . . .
pours old milk for an old cat.

Full-bodied and randomly young she clings,
peers down; hovers over a wine-filled vat,
and with outstretched arms like wings,
revels in the forming image of child below.

Despaired, she ripples a sunless finger
across the liquid eyes; in darkness
the child spirals down; drowns.
Pain leans her forward—face absorbing all—
mouth upon broken mouth, she drinks . . .

Within a delicate grey ruin
the vestal lady on Brattle
is up and about, as is her custom,
drunk with child.

THOUGHTS ON A
JAPANESE MOVIE

Let us love a thing together once
A thing vermilion

The plain is wide and many colors
Lie beneath the chestnut tree

Let us go there
You shall be my bride

I want to run vermilion through your hair

YOU CAME LAST SEASON

You came and made penny candies with your thumbs
I stole you and ate you
And my feet crushed your wrappers
            in a thousand streets
You hurt my teeth
You put pimples on my face
You were never anything for health
You were never too vitamin
You dirtied hands
And since you were stickier than glue
You never washed away
You stained something awful.

DEMENTIA IN AN AFRICAN APARTMENT HOUSE

A bullet-holed lion excited the dying child
    by yelping two-legged across the floor
    by scratching two-legged upon the door
The witch-doctor plugged his ears—the mother went wild!
The father came home the following year
    threw a week's purse with a curse
    into the witch-doctor's lap that couldn't hear
The wife sat in a corner scrubbing the skin of the lion.

"Make the bed! Make the bed!" he said.

She took the lion to another room
Came back; washed the blood from the door,
    put the dead child on the floor
And cleaned the sheets with a broom.

That night as the father lay sleeping
The wounded lion came in creeping;
The wife ran up to it, and on her knees fell:
"Lion, lion," she said, "my mind is not well."

CONEY ISLAND

1

Not so laughable this ocean that touches this fun-ruled shore,
Here the comedian-crab engulfs the sand,
commands the boardwalk, and strolls with an old-time joke.

And here the fungi-man comes to beach
humorless, leechy, hands to ground
with a pocketful of sun-tan lotion,
and he suns where the crab suns
tight beneath the merry-go-round.

Twin companions in search of a farce,
each giggling to each an inhuman scheme:
—Ah, yes! the feet of something dirty-big—
—The feet of everything dirty-big—
—The feet; nothing else—
—Just the feet. He-he-he-he-he-—

2

Night dips into an empty soda bottle,
and the joke wears off,
The fungi-man rolls up his beach towel
and drips away.

But not the comedian-crab . . .
tight beneath the sandy floor
The toe of a universe wiggles in its claw.
Tipsy-topsy
this scatter of feet drops into the sea
breaking into little bits broken men call broken ships.

3

Now here the sunken world of feetless men and women
ring-around-the-rosie men and women
hop-scotchers on the handle-bars
of imbeciles, inhuman—
flick on their neon-mockery of the stars
(noontime for the crab!)
thumbtacking their feet upon the sandy roof.

High tide and the hurry hurry houses
pull down their curtains
and the freaks slip out through back doors.
The rollercoaster and the ferris-wheel are standstill.
The mass silence deafens the last echo of a happy child.
The walky-goof comes with cantaloupe feet;
picks up the night-filled soda bottle
. . . and drinks . . .

In a usual morning zig-zag
exhausted crab greets fungi-man;

both sit crouched on the empty beach—waiting.

Both wondering what it could have been
that made this ocean decide this shore.

GREENWICH VILLAGE SUICIDE

Arms outstretched
hands flat against the windowsides
She looks down
Thinks of Bartok, Van Gogh
And New Yorker cartoons
She falls

They take her away with a Daily News on her face
And a storekeeper throws hot water on the sidewalk

IN THE MORGUE

I remember seeing their pictures in the papers;
Naked, they seemed stronger.
The bullet in my stomach proved that I was dead.
I watched the embalmer unscrew the glass top.
He examined me and smiled at my minute-dead-life
Then he went back to the two bodies across from me
And continued to unscrew.

When you're dead you can't talk
Yet you feel like you could.
It was funny watching those two gangsters across from me
              trying to talk.
They widened their thin lips and showed grey-blue teeth;

The embalmer, still smiling, came back to me.
He picked me up and like a mother would a child,
Rested me upright in a rocking chair.
He gave a push and I rocked.
Being dead didn't mean much.
I still felt pain where the bullet went through.

God! seeing the two gangsters from this angle was really
        strange!
They certainly didn't look like they looked in the papers.
Here they were young and clean shaven and well-shaped.

MY HANDS ARE A CITY

My hands are a city, a lyre
And my hands are afire
And my mother plays Corelli
      while my hands burn

SEA CHANTY

My mother hates the sea,

my sea especially,

I warned her not to;

it was all I could do.

Two years later

the sea ate her.

Upon the shore I found a strange

yet beautiful food;

I asked the sea if I could eat it,

and the sea said that I could.

—Oh, sea, what fish is this

so tender and so sweet?—

——Thy mother's feet—was its answer.

SONG

Oh, dear! Oh, me! Oh, my!
I married the pig's daughter!
I married the pig's daughter!

Why? Why? Why?

I met her in the evening
in the moon in the sky!
She kissed me in the evening
and wed me in her sty!
Oh, dear! Oh, me! Oh, my!
I married the pig's daughter!
I married the pig's daughter!

Why? Why? Why?

Because I felt I had oughta!
Because I was the one that taught her
how to love and how to die!
And tomorrow there'll be no sorrow
no, there'll be no sorrow
when I take her to the slaughter!
When I take her to the slaughter!

Why? Why? Why?

71

IN THE TUNNEL-BONE OF CAMBRIDGE

1

In spite of voices—
Cambridge and all its regions
Its horned churches with fawns' feet
Its white-haired young
        and ashfoot legions—
I decided to spend the night

But that hipster-tone of my vision agent
Decided to reconcile his sound with the sea
        leaving me flat
North of the Charles
                So now I'm stuck here—
                a subterranean
                lashed to a pinnacle

2

I don't know the better things that people know
All I know is the deserter condemned me to black—
He said: Gregory, here's two boxes of night
        one tube of moon
And twenty capsules of starlight, go an' have a ball—
He left and the creep took
        all my Gerry Mulligan records with him

3

But he didn't cut out right then
I saw him hopping
On Brattle street today—
            he's got a bum leg—
            on his way to the tunnel-bone
He made like he didn't see me
He was trying to play it cool

4

Wild in the station-bone
Strapped in a luggage vision-bone
            made sinister by old lessons of motion
The time-tablebone said: Black

Handcuffed to a minister
Released in a padded diesel
The brakeman punched my back: Destination, black

Out the window I could see my vision agent
            hopping along the platform
            swinging a burning-lantern-bone like mad
All aboard, he laughed, all aboard
Far into the tunnel-bone I put my ear to the ear
            of the minister—and I could hear
            the steel say to the steam
            and the steam to the roar: a black ahead
A black ahead a black and nothing more.

THE SHAKEDOWN

I spun another man's prayer
with the wind of my words
and another man's god
answered me with death.

It came in form of a mouth
and it kissed my mouth with breath.
Passionate breath; cold breath,
freezing my body in lifeless snow.

It floated before me, smiling;
and soon the sun appeared.
It melted me,
and the mouth knelt down to drink my terrible flow

VISION EPIZOOTICS

I see upon my bed
A mandrill sit,
It looks as if it's dead;
In fact, I'm sure of it.
It does not twitch its nose,
Nor does it blink!
And the marram in its toes
Long since began to stink.

From where it came, I'm at
A loss to say;
It's big and fierce and fat . . .
Too big to haul away.
What would explain its plan,
What mark or sign?
I looked and could not scan
beyond the mental line.

So I dreamed instead, and saw,
Still sitting dead,
The same I saw before:
The mandrill on my bed.
Awakened by the ice
Of its fur and thighs,
I caught it eating mice.

It smiled with shocking eyes,
And scratched its face and head
And then its knee.
"What do you want?" I said,
"What do you want of me?"
It smiled some more and wiped
Its rump with string
Of mouse and then it piped:
"Nothing, I want nothing."

NEW YORK MAN

He's come to Cambridge
He's standing behind my door
He's a New York man;
has big neon eyes
and his look spills
jazz upon the floor
But is he really there?
It could be a radio,
an organ grinder
hallucinating there.

It could well be me
paying me a visit in jazz,
afraid to knock.

IN THE EARLY MORNING

In the early morning
        beside the runaway hand-in-pocket
        whistling youth
I see the hopping drooling Desirer
His black legs . . . the corncob pipe and cane
The long greasy coat, and the bloodstained
    fingernails
He is waiting
        flat against the trees

KING CROW

Old crow is King Crow
He know all there is to know
Like when corn is ripe or when comes time to snow.
Old crow, he say: *Skee-ack!* like big
Thunder smack; and all crow
That is crow follow his long broken tail.

Scarecrow is Stuffed Crow, good crow
That stand all the time still
With old hat and leaky pail.
Scarecrow, he know Talako; he friend to great Wakonda!
And he know old crow is King Crow, and that all corn
is gold in old crow's land.

IN MY BEAUTIFUL . . . AND THINGS

All beautiful things
My things
In dead dogs in cellophane wrapped and tied
And still as beautiful as mine
In my tomb-rooms of dust and no things

A present practice of mine
When a beautiful chick passes by
To squeeze it thru my keyhole
Or slip it under the door if she's old
And not like a mother or a bitch

Or a motherless dog
Then I'll take her in my beautiful
And things
And will love her in cellophane with string
Like music for a world and no things

But I'm not proud with my dirty sink
And her things hanging on my doorknob to dry
It were better to be alone than a bitch
Housewifing my unwrapped dust
With nylons and sticks of tea and no things

DIALOGUES FROM CHILDREN'S OBSERVATION WARD

I

—You don't paint nice. You paint faces on window shades
and you don't make them look nice—

—Window shades is all I got,
and faces is all I got—

II

—Your mother came today. Did she say hello?—
—No—
—Did she see your black eye? Did she cry?
She gave you a box. What's in it?—
—A fox—
—Is it cooked? Can we eat it?
Is it silver or red?—
—It's not dead—
—Good! Yipeee! Let's kill it—
—She didn't even say, hello—

THE HORSE WAS MILKED

In a room a spoon upon the fire
was cooking his secret desire

When all was cooked he got a belt
and hurried before the horse could melt.

He strapped the belt across his arm;
wiped the needle so it'd not harm

and tightened, tightened the belt for a vein.
He pulled and his arm began to pain.

With steadied hand he waited the bulge—
waited the dream in which he'd indulge.

And it came, and the needle filled it with joy.
But the horse was milked, and there was no joy.

He fell to the floor without a sound,
and rolled his head like a merry-go-round.

Then he rubbed and shook and yanked his hair,
and vomited air, nothing but air.

Deep in the night he rolled and groaned.
O never was a poor soul so stoned.

THE CRIME

Into a burning animal his crime
raged its embittered stealth of humanness
and shook a young girl's laughter
with a deafening rush of animal-blood

Together they ate a rose
and together they dried their tongues
upon the ashes and remaining bits of fur

They loved and loved
until their eyes fell within them
and their faces fell away

THE SNIPER'S LAMENT

Hear beautiful
Hear through me still
There wasn't always this
And me with candles to sell
The Williamsburg Bridge could tell
Of the first b-b shot that missed
And accidentally hit the wax-factory
It hit in the sixth floor side
And granite and wax came out
And it still bleeds.

THIS IS AMERICA

This is America and I'm fun in it
with a wealth of music and lunatics
with a mouth that cannot sing
and I love a woman
and hate the rest and I'll make it
with anything female ten to fifty
and fifty's best
This is America and there's lots more
fun in it
and lunatics
lots that can't sing worth a damn
and lots that can
but who gives a damn
I do
In California I sang

my Eastern culture into a dying Mexican's ear
        that couldn't hear
and he died with a smile on his face
                The bastard had three gold teeth
        an ounce of tea
        a pocketful of payote
        and a fourteen year old wife

FRAGMENT FROM THE DECADENCE

Fortunato Giappinelli spat upon the rampart of Servius
        and urinated over the mountain ridges
            the Alpine pastures and the cypress and pine
                forests.
Bosco Totobocho saw this and did not like it
        So he climbed the Antonine Column and aimed his
        onager at the slob Fortunato Giappinelli
A Tuscan marble found its mark in Giappinelli's leg.
        He fell, and falling,
        helplessly urinated all over himself.
Bosco Totobocho howled with booms of laughter
        he rolled on the Alcantara over the Tagus
        holding his big belly booming and booming
        until he rolled right smack into a basilica
        and there the furious Giappinelli family
            awaited him.

THE GAME

Man Devil Mandrill—
Be the trinity of this so . . .
Then I shall lose this game
Of death to a pro.
I am too effete to compete
With you, sir;
You are a master and I, an amateur.
Pray sit, do not stir—
It would please, if not appease, me
No end if you were to spend
Some time with me
And I, the game, comprehend.
Now, am I right to assume
That there are set rules?
And that the game was never meant
To be played by fools?
Good. And am I also to assume
That if by chance I lose
It is your right to take from me
Whatever you see fit to choose?
Fair enough. Now then,
Let us begin,
And in due modesty,
May the better man win.

REQUIEM FOR
"BIRD" PARKER, MUSICIAN

this prophecy came by mail:
in the last murder of birds
a nowhere bird shall remain
and it shall not wail
and the nowhere bird shall be a slow bird
a long long bird
somewhere there is a room
in a room
in which an old horn
           lies in a corner
like a handful of rice
wondering about BIRD

          first voice

hey, man, BIRD is dead
they got his horn locked up somewhere
put his horn in a corner somewhere
like where's the horn, man, where?

          second voice

screw the horn
like where's BIRD?

third voice

gone
BIRD was goner than sound
broke the barrier with a horn's coo
BIRD was higher than moon
BIRD hovered on a roof top, too
like a weirdy monk he dropped
horn in hand, high above all
lookin' down on them people
with half-shut weirdy eyes
saying to himself: "yeah, yeah"
like nothin' meant nothin' at all

fourth voice

in early nightdrunk
solo in his pent house stand
BIRD held a black flower in his black hand
he blew his horn to the sky
made the sky fantastic! and midway
the man-tired use of things
BIRD piped a varied ephemera
a strained rhythmical rat
like the stars didn't know what to do
then came a nowhere bird

third voice

yeah, a nowhere bird—
while BIRD was blowin'
another bird came
an unreal bird
a nowhere bird with big draggy wings
BIRD paid it no mind; just kept on blowin'
and the cornball bird came on comin'

first voice

right, like that's what I heard
the draggy bird landed in front of BIRD
looked BIRD straight in the eye
BIRD said: "cool it"
and kept on blowin'

second voice

seems like BIRD put the square bird down

first voice

only for a while, man
the nowhere bird began to foam from the mouth
making all kinds of discords
"man, like make it somewhere else," BIRD implored

but the nowhere bird paced back and forth
like an old miser with a nowhere scheme

third voice

yeah, by that time BIRD realized the fake
had come to goof
BIRD was about to split, when all of a sudden
the nowhere bird sunk its beady head
into the barrel of BIRD's horn
bugged, BIRD blew a long crazy note

first voice

it was his last, man, his last
the draggy bird ran death into BIRD's throat
and the whole building rumbled
when BIRD let go his horn
and the sky got blacker . . . blacker
and the nowhere bird wrapped its muddy wings round BIRD
brought BIRD down
all the way down

fourth voice

BIRD is dead
BIRD is dead

first and second and third voices

yeah, yeah

        fourth voice

wail for BIRD
for BIRD is dead

        first and second and third voices

yeah, yeah

12 ASH ST. PLACE

That house is a ghost of pretty things;
like to the solitaire of a bird
a natural pity broods there.

There's an old man who always sits by candlelight.
I can see his hands move
dripping colors, crushed ones
like pressed flowers dropped from a book.

I passed his window one day;
got a closer look at him
. . . he must have been a hundred years old!
I asked him if he thought it would rain,
he said:—No—and dripped a purple color on my hand.

Walking away,
I told him I didn't think that was nice of him
. . . because the color burned.

THE WRECK OF THE NORDLING

One night fifty men swam away from God
And drowned.
In the morning the abandoned God
Dipped His finger into the sea,
Came up with fifty souls,
And pointed towards eternity.

MAN SEATED OUTSIDE MY WINDOW

Time on a garden's wintry quietness
means nothing when you find
you're watching the seasons go by alone;
means nothing when you find
your finger marking your thoughts upon a stone.

YOU, WHOSE MOTHER'S LOVER
WAS GRASS

You, whose mother's lover was grass in the greenest season,
shall be born bastard in his warm green hands
and he shall be ephemeral
and shall not have enough time to teach you sun
     and rain and wind,
yet you shall rock rock in his warm green hands
until the jealous season murders him.
And winter does come!
You shall not be old enough to walk
     to crush the snow that buries him;
your mother shall carry you upon her head
hold you close to wind
and the wind shall brool within your ear
a place where no grass grows
The slowest of clouds shall be your mother's guide.
She shall follow them
     fog-led to an asphalt flight
where, at journeys end,
you shall be orphaned to an asphalt city . . .
and there no grass shall grow, and no cloud remain.
Your mother—your mother shall return to another season,
to another grass lover, and her lover will not endure.
Winter pursues your mother for his own;
his jealousy makes bastards of us all.

AN OLD MAN SAID HE ONCE SAW EMILY DICKINSON

Unhappy face—tight rich white face

Like a beautiful dead woman's face—She looked at me.

Her long hands were wrapped around her throat

And her silk-black hair hung like sleeping bats;

It wasn't me she was looking at.

When I walked away I could still see her looking there

. . . But nothing was there;

That is, nothing that I could see.

THE RUNAWAY GIRL

Ever since running away from home
somebody real weird tailed her;
it's been her constant paranoia.
Like a bug, it hugs close to the ground.
And no matter where she walks, it follows her.

In the distance behind her
she can hear her mother calling, calling;
yet she cannot turn around.

INTO THE APERTURE OF AN
UNLIKELY ARCHIMAGE

On coming past a thing of hand
autochthonic like dirt my hand
touching the thing I hold most
going walking and passing gone
tired again because rain again
because all that's not flesh is
not old in walking so walk again
and pass light into a passing sheet
used to sleep and woman while walking

Make it all pass and hold sleep well
as a man might there ain't none often
enough to reverberate the mammoth yet
on coming past arm in arm with woman
as a thing to hold most mostly and I
like anyone could be good with sleep
held again because rain agains sleeps
Gone and bright youths gladiate head
thrusts forward toward man's future
malobservation hung-up on Kant
locked in impure planispiral rajyoga
when all that really matters is sleep
and having babies with a big smile like

scrimshaw the dabblings on a whale's tooth
by some cornball sailor afraid to Harvard
yard his walk or praise Caligula for his green thumb
morning past morning past on coming past

Wonderful these are the tired things
the rush and the well of life moving
Leave it to the subkingdom the phylum
the purple senescence of young America
leave it and go on coming past touching
the thing you hold most and now sleep

A PASTORAL FETISH

Old Mac Donald wears clod-hoppers
in his walk through field of lilac and dandelion
A storm-trooper, like a Klee twittering machine, he stomps:
Crunch one lilac here; crunch another dandelion there,
here, there, everywhere (he's got no mercy at all)
crunch crunch here and a crunch crunch there
crunch everywhere . . . .

There comes a time when he's got to stop
take off his shoes; go to bed . . .
ah, that's when Old MacDonald's in his glory.
Green blood and mud-caked leather he digs the most.
He makes it a habit to sleep his nose by his toes
so that all night long he could snore in the sticky smell
of murdered lilac and dandelion.
It's the old bastard's greatest kick.

THE SAUSAGES

I ate sausages with you at the feast.
I ate sausages, and across the street
the butcher counted his daughter's feet!

ST. LUKES, SERVICE FOR THOMAS

The White Horse innkeeper
Leaned nervously against the stained-glass;
He shifted his feet, and Cummings mourned by.

A sightseer whispered into a sightseeing ear.
And a Swansea woman entered. . .

Two neon-villagers underarmed her;
Sat her down in the first row.
She raised her head, and peered
. . . The body wasn't there.

The service ended in illimitable whispers.

A Ceylonese prince was first to leave.
He waited by the church gate
And little groups gathered, chattered.

Across the street the school children
Were playing tag-ball.
The ball rolled in front of the innkeeper;
He kicked it hard
And strode back to his inn.

CAMBRIDGE, FIRST IMPRESSIONS

1

It is not easy to walk
    these Cambridge streets
Better carpets make it difficult.

Yet in masquerade I slip unnoticed within the parade
And my walk is slightly eased.
How great it is to be heralded in walking!

But my lie makes awkward the gait.
Out of step, my identity is revealed.
The ash-foot sentinels
    on every Cambridge corner
    stand too severe;
Their clarion-warnings discord
    the rhythms I walk to hear.

2

Yet Cambridge is not all banner and majesty,
On the side lines
    I watch the rhythmic embassy—
    Brattle and all its accoutrements—

Give up their rigid themes
Forsake their regnant march
Roll up the carpets,
     go home.

Home, and the streets are unnatural.
Walking, I catch Cambridge in a seldom jubilee:—
     Vivaldi, Getz, Bach and Dizzy,
     in a melody all together contained,
     emerge, like twining wisps of smoke,
     from out parlors and cellars,
Jumping the chestnuts in Longfellow;
Sprinting down Hawthorne,
Swinging through Lowell,
And flying real-crazy over Dana.

3

Morning, and it is terrible to walk.
Once again the sentinels are stationed;
     their clarions pied-pipe
     the streets clean of the jubilant night-rats,
And quickly the better carpets spread.

4

The old bastard lied that told me Melville
     visioned lots of times while walking

in the early morning,
      separate from the carpets and parade, on Brattle.
I've walked Brattle lots these days,
      and not once did I catch from out the dark
      a line of light.

He said:—Walk, man, walk that crazy Revolutionary road,
      old Brattle;
You'll dig the greatest visions ever;
Man, like Melville visioned Moby Dick right on Brattle!
Right in the middle of the street!

5

Tired of walking,
Tired of seeing nothing,
I look out from a window
      belonging to someone
      nice enough to let me look.

And from a window Cambridge is not all that bad.
It is a great feeling to know
      that from a window
I can go to books to cans of beer to past loves.
And from these gather enough dream
      to sneak out a back door.